WONDER
STARTERS

Snow

Pictures by BERMEJO

Published by WONDER BOOKS
A Division of Grosset & Dunlap, Inc.
51 Madison Avenue   New York, N.Y. 10010

About Wonder Starters

Wonder Starters are vocabulary controlled information books for young children. More than ninety per cent of the words in the text will be in the reading vocabulary of the vast majority of young readers. Word and sentence length have also been carefully controlled.

Key new words associated with the topic of each book are repeated with picture explanations in the Starters dictionary at the end. The dictionary can also be used as an index for teaching children to look things up.

Teachers and experts have been consulted on the content and accuracy of the books.

Published in the United States by Wonder Books, a Division of Grosset & Dunlap, Inc.

Library of Congress Catalog Card Number 74-2753
ISBN: 0-448-09682-X (Trade Edition)
ISBN: 0-448-06418-9 (Library Edition)

FIRST PRINTING 1974

Printed and bound in the United States.

It's winter.
There is a lot of snow.
We're throwing snowballs.

1

The snow is cold.
My gloves keep my hands warm.
I'm wearing warm clothes.

2

Our toboggan goes very fast.
It slides down the slope.
The runners slide on the snow.

Skis slide on snow, too.
These boys are skiing.

4

The boys have skied down the slope.
The ski lift pulls them up again.

This is a ski jump.
Men can jump a long way on skis.

6

This man is skiing between the flags.
He tries to go very fast.
This is a slalom race.

It's snowing.
Snowflakes have six points.
They are beautiful.

The wind is blowing hard.
The wind blows the snow.
This is a snowstorm.

The snowstorm has stopped.
Everything is under snow.
There are deep snowdrifts.
Cars get stuck in snowdrifts.
10

The snowplow
clears the road.
Men dig the cars out.

When it gets warmer
the snow thaws.
The snow turns into slush
and water.
12

Sometimes snow slides
down the mountainside.
This is called an avalanche.

Some places are always cold.
The snow never thaws.
People use snow to build houses.
The houses are called igloos.
14

It is hard to walk on snow.
These men wear snowshoes.
Snowshoes help when walking on snow.

15

Reindeer live in cold places.
Their big hoofs
help them to walk on the snow.
16

walrus

husky

weasel

polar bear

These animals live in
snowy places, too.
Many of them are white
like the snow.

North Pole

South Pole

At the earth's poles there is only
ice and snow.
Sometimes explorers go there.
18

It is always cold
on mountaintops.
The snow hardly ever melts.

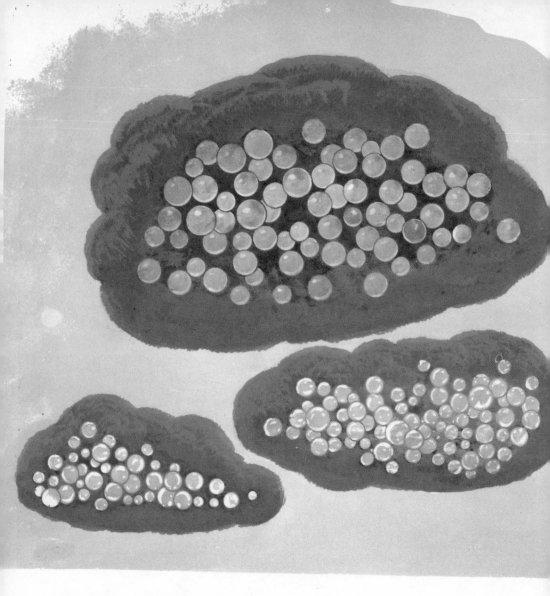

Snow comes from clouds.
Clouds are made of many
drops of water.
20

When it is very cold,
the water turns to ice.
The pieces of ice
fall as snowflakes.

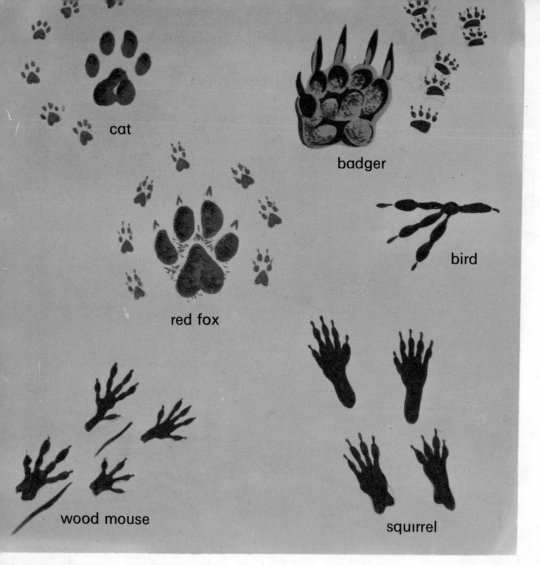

cat

badger

bird

red fox

wood mouse

squirrel

See for yourself.
Sometimes you can see
animal tracks in the snow.
Here are some animal tracks.

22

Starter's **Snow** words

snowball
(page 1)

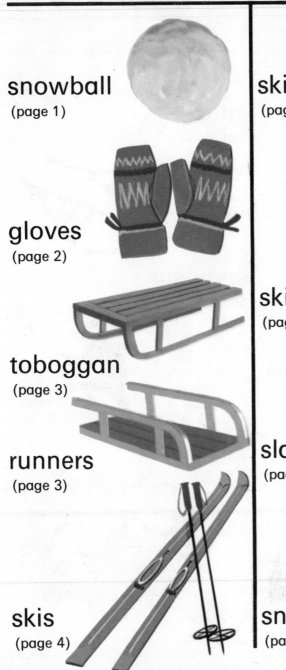

gloves
(page 2)

toboggan
(page 3)

runners
(page 3)

skis
(page 4)

ski lift
(page 5)

ski jump
(page 6)

slalom
(page 7)

snowflake
(page 8)

23

snowstorm

(page 9)

igloo

(page 14)

snowdrift

(page 10)

snowshoe

(page 15)

snowplow

(page 11)

explorer

(page 18)

avalanche

(page 13)

24

track

(page 22)